WELCOME HOME
DEAR SOUL

Tasmin Hansmann

WELCOME HOME
DEAR SOUL

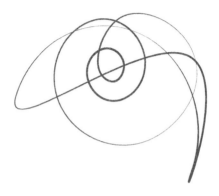

For the roots of my family tree

Welcome home, dear soul.

Welcome to the realm of nothing, a place of no restrictions. The fire you see is from all the witches you burned and the wings on your back have grown from all the love you have given.

It is good to see you again, dear soul.

Let me show you around.

After all this time,
every time you are re-entering this place, you forget who I am.

It is so interesting to see. Sometimes you welcome me with a
smile, sometimes you scream in fear.

But always, always,
you carry grief within you before life leaves you.

And surprise upon my arrival.

Yes, I am a woman.

Or at least what you define as one.

I am glad that in this life you finally understood
that gender does not matter at all.
That the shes and hes and theys and thems are all valid and a
part of the same river that humanity tries to divide into lakes.
They will forever fail as this is a task only gods can fulfil.

And we do not want to.

You were created like us, fluid and liquid
and everything in between,
loving everyone or no one and sometimes a bit too much.

I am not a she or a they, but you can call me that, if that is
easier for you to say. But I am nothing and all the same.

Pronouns are a thing of human minds,
they mean nothing to gods like us.

I speak your language, as I speak every human language that
ever touched history's tongue and every language of the animal
and plant kingdom, as you are all kin, all made from the same
energy. But yes, that lesson will come to you soon enough.

Made of shadows, I am surprised my gender is always the most interesting part humans notice.

No animal has ever asked me for my name or the curves of my presence. All they see are shadows and magic and they bow or hiss or watch carefully.

You, however, human soul, you still have a lot to learn.

Look at me and look closely.

I am transformation.

Nothing of my shape ever remains the same.

Flames licking between fingers that are disappearing and changing into claws, horns growing and tangling until they have become antlers made of echoes. Eyes made of lava, melting away the humanity your dying eyes try to see. Just my scythe remains the same, formed of basalt, the most holy of all, the only material worthy of death.

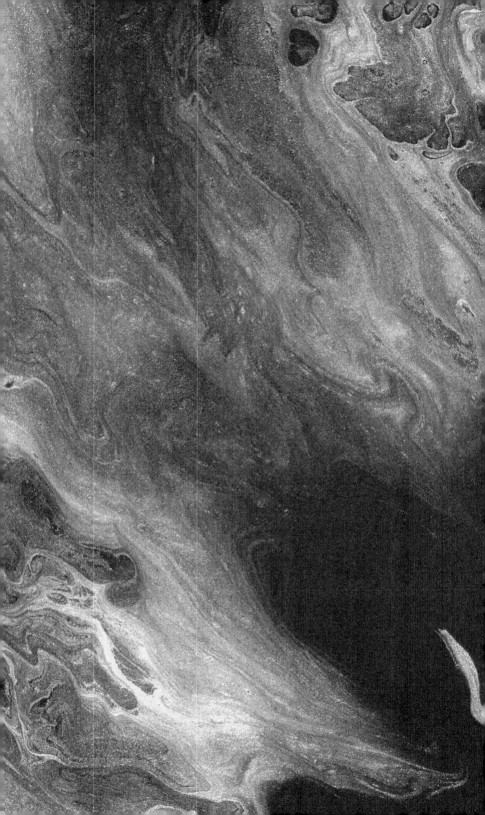

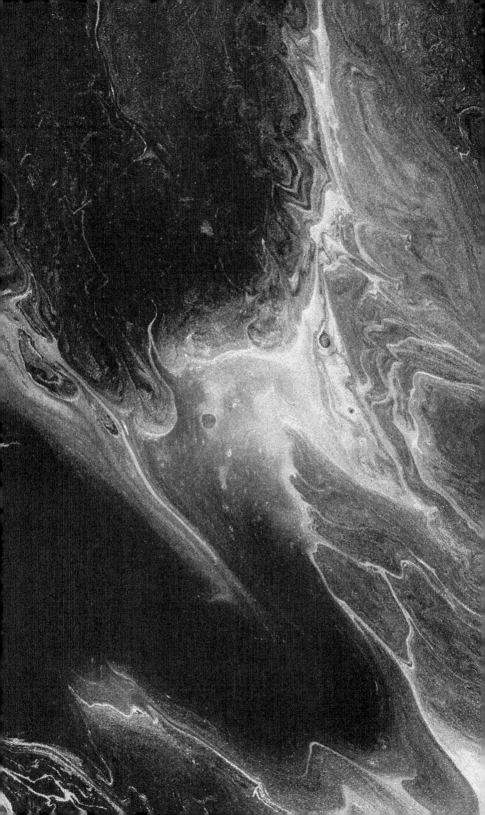

You gave me many names over the continents and centuries.

Azrael, Mictecacihuatl, Hades, Jabru, Yama, Odin, Osiris, Anubis, Ereshkigal, Maweth, Śmierć, Giltiné, Dea Tacita, Batara Kala, Shinigami, Asto Cidatu, Tuoni, Pana, Supay, Hel and so many more.

Some simply call me Death, without a face attached, which I appreciate. You may also call me Demon or Devil or simply God or Goddess, it is all fine by me.

At the end of the day, I do not care.

When I am called upon I always know, no matter which words are used. Most of the time they are not used at all.

There is no need of words when a soul is leaving the place it called home.

It is a silence that calls me like a curse, like a blessing.

Whenever one heartbeat disappears, I will be there, devouring the emptiness of sound and welcoming you here.

Rituals are entertaining, I do enjoy watching them.

Some of them are truly delightful, others are clearly only meant to soothe the grieving human mind and that is okay, too. But respecting deities is important, you see.

As big as you can be, there is always something bigger,
someone you cannot control,
something you do not understand.

It is important to accept the unknown, the powerful,
the mighty above all.

We may only be a mirror of nature, a mirror of all things alive, but that is already so much more than one single being could ever understand.

To burry a body,
to mourn in pain,
to pray,
to sing,
to celebrate ashes and bodies and the memory,

those are things that remind you
of your part in the picture.

You are not the picture.
You are a drop of paint on a canvas as big as the universe.
And still, without you, it would be incomplete.

The masterpiece may always be changing, it will never be
done, souls dying and life creating, but yet your presence is
significant and barely noticeable just the same.

There are people missing you right now. Let's have a look, dear soul, what they have to say. Let's read the script of their hearts.

Follow me and look closely, listen to the flow of emotions, guided by the rhythm of their heartbeats.

Let's start with your neighbour.

Oh, yes, of course you are surprised. You did not know
him very well, did you?
The name written on the doorbell and on letters
accidentally brought to you is a familiar sound and yet he
remained a stranger in all those years.

He does not know how to feel about your death. He is
asking if we should mourn humans we barely knew. Who
remained on the sidelines of our own lived experience.
But then again, he saw you almost every single day, a
consistent reminder of the fact that people may not share
love or lives but the same space as us.
You were a part of his life, even though your bond was not
strong. Sometimes emotions are not the only thing that
connects us to one another.

He remembers the way you treated the flowers in your
garden with grace. You had no idea what you were doing,
you simply enjoyed their presence, but he does not know
that. He only saw them bloom and waited for spring every
year. He is wondering what will happen to your cat, he
has not seen him in a while. He never liked your furry
companion, but now he thinks of taking him in, so he can
stay in the place he has always lived in.

There is a flower of kindness and compassion
blooming in him, do you see?

It is still a little seed,
but it will transform the landscape of his soul.

Loss changes people, dear soul,
it makes us grow in ways we barely see.

So, watch closely.
Learn, while you are in this place, unable to feel.

If you are still human now that you are with me?

Well, have you ever been human
in the first place, my dear?

Do not get confused, we are no longer in the place you lived in during your last chapter of life.

We are traveling, even though for gods traveling is something we do not do.

We simply are.
Whenever, wherever.

But I respect that your mind processes time and space differently, so let me just say that we are far away now, somewhere you have never been to in your lifetime.
I could tell you the name of the country, but names and borders change so fast and mean nothing to the essence of everything that is important.

I quite like that about the living beings.
All their different concepts of distances and time.

I love to communicate with the trees when they die,
their view on the world is always refreshing, as their only
movement is up into the sky and deep down into the soil.
They connect worlds that otherwise would barely touch.

Humans can do this too, but not physically. You can bring
together art or hate in ways that are so new to the world
that it can save and destroy them in a single breath.

All living things hold power,
but none underestimate others like humans do.

If you would be more like the trees in the way you move
through your minds and invisible threads of togetherness,
maybe you would even threaten the gods with your
creativity.

But we know we do not need to worry.

Now, look into the realm of life.

Do you recognize this face?

This, my dear soul,
is the face of a person that you broke into pieces.

I give you a few moments to think again who that person is. You know her, trust me.

.   .   .

Your childhood friend, exactly.

She looks different now, doesn't she? Moved thousands of miles across the globe and still she is the same child you loved so much growing up. She is unaware that she still carries this kind of innocence in her heart, like she used to long before... well, life happened.

She does not trust people, but she tries.

Why, you ask?

Well, if material things would exist in this realm, I would tell you to look into a mirror. But that mirror would be empty right now, so it is pointless.

You are the reason she does not trust people.

When she heard that you were joking about her constant singing, calling her annoying and her voice unbearable, she was devastated.
She has never known that you were just trying to make friends at school, unaware of the consequences, just learning from the poison that spilled out of other people's mouths.

You did not mean it.

You thought she would never know. But she did. She thought she was safe with you, a place where she could be herself. She broke her guitar that night, not picking up another instrument for years.

You didn't know, life had carried you away from her, your mind innocent but your actions carving scars into another human soul. She spent some time in the high mountains, found her spirituality and learned to listen to the silent echoes of the wind.

Did you know that storms carry
the songs of gods and goddesses?

She knows and so, even after all these years, she woke up
tonight. Only stars looking down on her and yet she knew
that you left, never to return.

She made her peace with what you did and if you look
closely, you can see music filling the cracks in her heart,
forming a new song inspired by your absence.

Let's go back, shall we?

I am opening doors in your mind that should remain shut, as your time with me is limited. Time might work differently here than you would ever understand, but we need to keep moving.

I cannot fix the structures of how life works for you, human soul, so we have to move on.

You are never invincible,
even when you do not exist anymore.

There will always be limits for you,
as you are human and nothing
like the deities that watch over you.

Yes, we do care.

But we also do not.

One day, you will understand.

Look.
We are back where we started. Your hometown of choice.

Your boss has just learned about your passing.
Oh, how he hated you.

Still, he is upset, he needs to find another employee
that will do your work. It will be a few weeks before the
business runs smoothly again.

Can you feel the rage? Hot and sharp, cutting through his
own happiness. Capitalism is like a plague, dear human
one, one that is almost impossible to heal as you are blind
for the symptoms.
His greed makes him hungry, power makes him numb.

The only thing he feels when he thinks of you now is anger
about the wasted time at the funeral and the financial
expenses of training someone else.

Cruel souls always exist and yet,
they were still children once upon a time.

Every villain has the potential of innocence in them. The
same way even good people carry blossoms of evil within.

No, he does not miss you.
But he will continue to speak about you.
He will remember you.

Do you see now that the people who carry your legacy are
not always kind to you? How every person that has ever
met you sees a different version of you?

None of them are true and yet they still define who you
are. You are made up of perceptions and perspectives,
opinions and experiences. The good and the bad and
everything in between.

You are a kaleidoscope of yourself,
carried into the future by others
who only ever got a glimpse of you,
just like you only got a glimpse of them,
always thinking you had the best view.

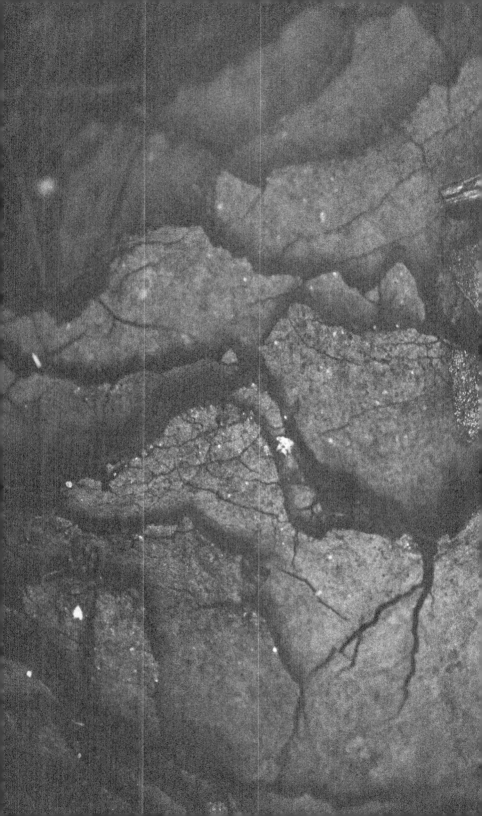

I will not make you see the grief of the ones closest to you.

You would not be able to cope with the vast emptiness in their soul, the grief that consumes every particle of their being, the darkness that overshadows every ray of light there was.

You might not feel while you are with me,
but the destruction of grief is too all-consuming
for your mind to handle.

Grief is an essential part of your lived experience, dear human one, but to feel the grief about your own passing from everyone that loves you dearly… oh, it would break you into endless pieces of pain.

And I do not have time to reconstruct you, my dear soul.

Humans have a way of shaping the world around them,
including all living things.

You are shapeshifters,
have always been.

And even though it is the most obvious thing about you,
you tend to not realize it about yourselves.

You mold and mend the hearts, energies and circumstances
with every breath, every word, every action. To the positive
and the negative and everything in between.

Your stories of Old and the stories of New are always full
of magic, of witches and wizards and light bringers and
shadow creatures.

You dream of fantastical worlds,
not realizing how powerful the magic is
that every single one of you possesses.

The power of change.
The power to shape the world around you
in the most subtle and impressive ways.
The power to make someone love you
by just existing.
Or hate you.

Either way
mountains are moved
for a person you feel strongly about.

The closest you get to this awareness is when you lose
someone you love.

Suddenly, there is a wound, like someone has ripped out
a part of yourself that never physically existed. The magic
is gone and the gaping hole it leaves behind makes you
hungry and mourning and restless.

That is when you see how much impact a single person has
on you, even if this person was not close to you or had so
many flaws, you had no idea why you still let them be a
part of your life.
And yet there you were, holding back tears for this other
soul that is no longer by your side, over and over again.

But still, you do not realize that every word you say, every action you do, has consequences for the very fabric of the universe. You are blind in ways you cannot even dream of.

The echo of yourself will always be heard in the valley
of time, an ever repeated footprint, losing its power the
further it travels but it will always remain.
A signature in the invisible, carried on by the world,
unaware of your existence.

You do not need to be king or queen to form an empire of memories. Your name does not need to last to leave a mark.

Even when the living realm forgets,
we gods will always remember.

Your ancestors?

Well, we will get to that later.

Let me just say that it is good to remember the ones who passed on. No matter if you are related in DNA, experience or other connections, the humans that formed the path your soul was able to walk on, are an important part of who you are and who you have become.

It is your duty to remember.
To celebrate.
To praise.
To question.
To make things better.

To become one of them, when it is your time to leave.

I am one of the few certainties in your life.
The fact that we meet on the day you leave the world you knew behind, is a given. No amount of trying or hoping or praying will change that. It has been like that forever and will continue on until time itself has enough of all of us.

So, dear soul, you see, grief will always haunt you, no matter how far you run. You lose yourself every day a little bit more and so does everyone else. You will have to say goodbye, no matter how much you try.

If you are an infant who only survives a day you still have lost something. Your own chances, your own opportunities and the parents you just met.

When you grow old and survive all things terrible and wonderful, you will have buried too many dreams and loved ones for one heart to carry.

Loss is the soil to your roots.

There is so much more lost than found. But isn't that the beauty of life, dear human one? It leaves the doors open for exploration and venture. For growth and blossom.

Maybe that is why you forget about my existence. If you'd know what came next, if you knew that I am waiting here on the doorstep of the realm of darkness, maybe grief would not humble you.

But then again, maybe you do know.

Otherwise, I would not be known, with whatever name came to mind. You make death into a person, you let it be executed by a reaper, you imagine a guardian of all souls lost, a god or goddess to offer sacrifices to. You pray for gentleness, for forgiveness, for absolution.

I am your first and final transformation.

Maybe a part of me travels with you,
wherever you may go.
My soft touch just one fatal mistake
or one horrifying twist of fate away.

I am always gentle but grief never is.

As for the absolution, we gods do not forgive nor do we judge. You are as you are. We may shape the consequences of your being, but there is no personal emotion attached.

We value life. In all its forms and variations. In all colours of mischief and glory and kindness and horror.

It is not our place to forgive as we will never suffer from your mistakes. It is truly human to think anyone else could carry your burden for you. There is no one but yourself.

There can be no forgiveness
without an honest apology, my dear.

And we do not need your apologies,
we know every intention and feeling you ever had, as
confusing or complex it might have been. We see the truth,
therefore we do not need words or tears or promises.
But other people do.

Live for the humans, not for the gods.

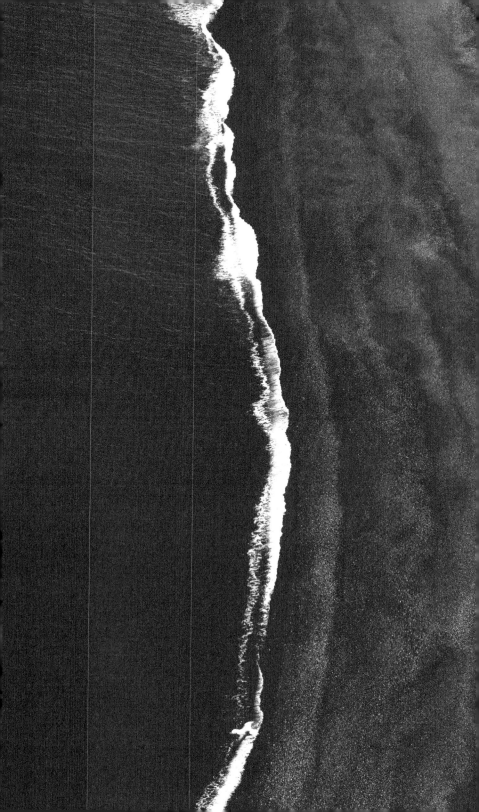

Demons or saints, they are mortals after all.

Melancholy and magic flow through them like rivers through valleys, carving a new landscape out of the bare nothingness of moments that have long passed.

Do you hear their songs?
Do you hear them sing?
Does the melody of their power radiate through you?

Guitar strings, lonely saxophones at night,
fingers on piano keys, drums in the distance.

Demons and saints, my dear.
You never had to choose.

If in this life you would have chosen art, you maybe would have seen what the universe is truly made of.

The fabric of humanity, the colours of storms and the symphonies of the silence between the trees.

You would have seen, spoken, screamed, dreamed of nothing but the delicate web of possibilities.

Everything can be something, if you just let it be.

But just as all these possibilities, you might learn this lesson when the cycle repeats itself.

We will see, human one, we will see.

I would like to show you something.

Something that you know,
something that has been with you your entire life.

                                        Come with me.

Perspective is key when it comes to the most important things in life. So, let me help you understand by becoming impossible for just a few moments.

This is your planet.

Do you understand now?
Seeing this blue marble from far away.
Do the dimensions make sense now? Do you recognize the miracle that is this place? Do you see your neighbouring planets, the asteroids, the moon and the little burning life giver in the distance that is so huge and yet so small in the comparison of all things space.

And now look closely,
we are seeing the smallest living things in their variety.

These are not atoms or neutrons or quarks, or however
your scientists call the core nowadays,
we do not have time for that.
These are simply the smallest creatures
that make life possible.

Yes, your life, my dear soul.

And that of every single being you have ever met, no
matter if you considered it a human or something beneath
you. You are all equals.

And by hurting one, you are hurting everybody else.

The scale of what is defined as alive is endless and way beyond your understanding.

Yet you try to destroy the very foundation of your home. I always worried about those suicidal tendencies. You rattle and burn with your eyes closed, poisoning your own waters, setting your own lungs ablaze.

You do not even know life and yet you seem to have a love affair with death and destruction. You have a desire, a hunger for me and my darkness.
I have to disappoint you, it is not mutual. I feel many things, but not a single one is a human emotion that would make sense to you. I also do not share.

Death is who I am, you are simply allowed to witness its sensation. Your longing for my power does not suit you. It will hunt and haunt you.

Maybe one day we will need to wake you up.
        But then again, we try not to interfere with you.

The teachers are always quiet during a test, like some of
you humans like to say. And believe me when I say that
even if you fail, the planet will still be here, recovering,
patiently.

Millions of years are nothing for life itself, as time does
not exist for things like creation. Only dictated by the slow
heavy seconds of a star in the centre of your system. Or the
black hole in the centre of your galaxy, depending on who
gets hungry first.

You, however, do not have the luxury of eternal grace,
human one.

        You need the planet. It does not need you.

        Remember that. Remember it well.

Open your third eye now, my dear soul.

I always have to remind you when you come home.
One day you might arrive and immediately expand your
senses to what the human body cannot feel.

Look at the energies flowing.

You exchange much more with the world than just your
breath, your sound and your physical body.
You yourself are more than noise and flesh. There is an
energy to all things, floating in fine constellations.

You see, many authors and philosophers and scientists and developers have asked themselves when something is considered alive.

While energy is always present, there are certain things in this world that only absorb and do not give back. Your phones, laptops and all those grey buildings you erect into the sky, those do only take, take and take.

Reciprocity is what makes you a being of life.

Go ask a gardener, a nomad, a wanderer, a healer.
They know.
You know.

The kinder you are, the more alive you become, no matter if you find the right words or make money.
A currency does not exist in the truth of reality, but an ongoing flow of energy does.

If you do not radiate back the love you receive, in whatever shape or form, you block the flow. If you do not accept help or kindness from others, you block the flow. If you are not kind to yourself, you block the flow.

You are a vessel.
You yourself are a river of energy within an ocean of life
Keep moving, do not be still.
You were never meant to be stable.
You were always meant to be wild and ever changing.
Be the love, be the energy, be in motion.

Why I am showing these things to you?

Because you need to be prepared to forget.

And the day you learn those lessons the hard way,
it will feel like coming home.

The echo of your memory will be there,
waiting for you to realize the truth
of what makes you you.

Energy and love are synonyms,
yet they are not the same.

You cannot love someone without an exchange of
energy. But just because there is an exchange of energy
does not mean that there is love. And just because you
love someone, or something does not mean the flow is
undisrupted.

Some humans love so blindly, it is painful to watch,
even for a goddess like me. It makes my decisions
and my conversations with you so much harder.

When someone has led their life filled with good intentions without even realizing how egocentric their behaviours have been. When you think that you sacrifice yourself for love, but all you do is sacrifice others for the love of yourself.

You strangle people with what you call love, even though it is a toxic poison only brewed to feed you with the nectar of other peoples affirmations, acceptance and affection.

When you love the bird so much you never let it fly out of fear of it falling from the sky.

You have done this too, human one, but luckily this time
around it was only in a few circumstances.

When you loved someone so much you did not let them go
because you couldn't bear the thought of being alone.
You know who I am talking about.
I might be almighty, but you are not dumb, you still have
your memories from your past life.

I do not have to explain your own truth to you, do I?

Just rip off the curtain of excuses and scratch away the
paint of lies you created to feel safe and protected.

You are dead.
There is no safer space than your own grave.

Only brave and good people know when to let someone move on. When it is the time to say your goodbyes, to turn away, regardless of the pain and loneliness it causes.

You did that when your mother passed. You offered her the freedom to leave. You made peace, opened the door to the silence of my realm. You gave her this present, as a last act of love, although she had never given you this kind of love in return. She was an example of the type of person with good intentions but a heart so heavy, its gravitational pull almost destroyed you growing up. She wanted nothing more but to be loved by you, to see you grow up, so you could make her happy, that she tried to cut your wings whenever you even moved your feathers. There was no room to breathe, let alone fly.

As I do not judge, it is up to you to decide if this was something bad she did. If that is what you call love or narcissism.

These decisions were yours to make
while your were one of the living.

Now you are one with me and the time of your judging has passed. Now you are the one moving on. There is no return and some decisions will forever be undone.

There are a few more things I would like to talk about before I must return to my duty of keeping watch over the fields of shadows within a bright and shining world. To look for the end of all options within a whole planet of possibility.

I want you to know that the note you found on your sister's desk when she was sixteen has saved her life.

Suicide is nothing shameful but it is a shortcut and an end to all the versions of yourself you could still become. There is always hope, even when it hides in the most impossible corners filled with nothing but darkness.

You had seen the hope she was unable to find. You guided her soul to a safe space where she was able to open her eyes to the possibility of survival. You never knew that this note was meant to become a goodbye letter to all of you. But you sensed that she needed you to be there and simply show her, that being alive was worth a try.

I will welcome her here one day
but I am glad that you are the first one to arrive.

Me? Morbid?

My darling, I am death.

I am demon.
I am void.
I am the opposite of all things holy.
I am the end of all energy.
I am the end of everything and everyone.

I am the end of you.

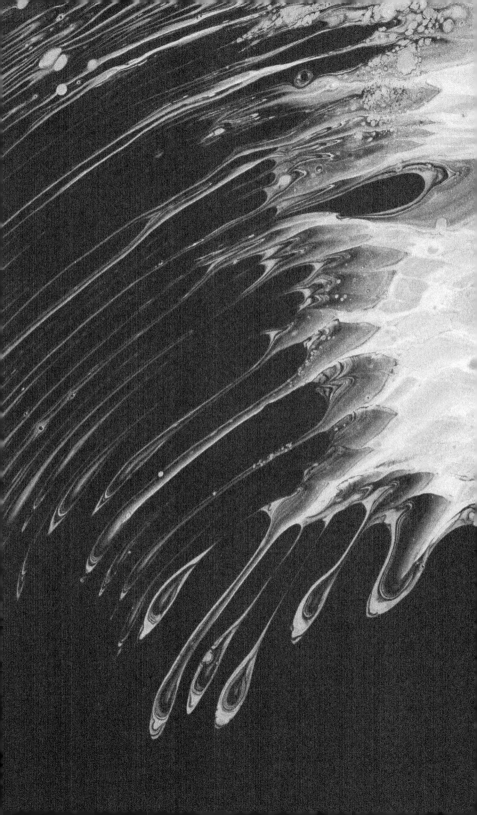

You are having a good point.

If I am demon, this should be hell.

But I am also goddess, so this should be heaven.

Well, my dear soul, you would be surprised to learn that my realm is neither. But that you have been to both.

Heaven and hell exist.
As one.

It is the Earth that is your paradise as well as the burning gates of eternal doom. All the names of different religions and faiths for what you call Heaven and Hell are simple synonyms for life on earth.

Everything is equally dangerous and promising, horrible and wonderful.

A family builds their dream house on stolen land with invisible blood on their hands, slowly choking the joy out of people they will never meet.

A person enjoys the best dinner they have ever tasted while the home of the animal on his plate is fed to the flames and leaves nothing but ashes.

The guardians of the rainforest celebrate a victory to protect a piece of land that was their native home, being one with the ritual and nature, while somewhere in an office building not too far away someone takes their medication against mental illness caused by the very system that was supposed to uplift them.

A man enjoys a wonderful evening while the woman next to him is having the worst night of her life.

Someone wakes up, beaten and sore, while a thief runs away with happy tears as his grandmothers disease can be treated with a strangers money.

An author celebrates their debut book that will bring change and joy to people while somewhere else one lights a fire in a forest that will be turned into paper.

A black woman breaks the walls of oppression in a country ruled by white men and finally gets the promotion and acknowledgement that she deserves while her cousin serves unjust jail time and suffers from trauma.

A homeless person feels gratitude upon the few dollars that will pay them a warm meal tonight, while a rich person walking past has just lost their son because no money on earth could keep me away.

Somewhere close to a desert one finds miracles upon the wildlife, while just across an invisible boarder, children are taken from their home, never to be seen again.

Some community finds ecstasy, belonging and peace in prayer while the queer kid in their middle will one day be murdered by one of them.

A trans person finally feels their freshly operated chest, feeling relief and delight no one can describe, while in the refugee camp a teenager dies of a simple cold leaving a family grieving that has already lost everything they had left after years of terror.

In a beautiful barn on the outscrits of a city a disabled person marries the love of their life, while halfway across the globe someone falls into a coma that will damage their brain beyond repair.

In the same hospital, a few rooms away, a mother births her long awaited child and welcomes new life into the world, while a few miles from this miracle a couple gets denied the right to adopt and is left with all the love they wanted to give, shattered into pieces.

On a sunny island, people find resilience in their ancient cultural traditions, while somewhere across the horizon the waters are drenched with the blood of sharks, dolphins and all types of fish, the ecosystem destroyed.

Above your head, someone enters the ISS and fulfills their dreams, while on the poles the ice melts under the scientists and animals feet, opening a void no one can close.

In this very moment, someone has the first kiss of their life, feeling love and excitement, while someone else breaks under violence and will never recover. Someone orgasms, another has an accident. Some suffer, some cry with joy.

It all happens.

Now.

Just open your eyes and you will see.

There is no such thing as separation.

Life after death is a myth.

There is life.

And there is death.

Like day and night.
Your time as an individual on the planet is unique.

Why would you live and then die and continue to live?
There is no reason in that.
We gods may adore chaos but we also adore logic.

You get one chance - or I should say one life with many
chances? Sometimes, if you are lucky, you greet me and I
let you return if there is a reason you need to be saved.

But once you enter my realm with your entire soul,
the life you knew ended.

There would be no reason in dying if you would continue to be the same person, just living in another dimension.

Human souls always think
there will be salvation and something else.
More, more, more.

The next best thing or the next worst thing.

Never enough, never an end.

A part of you may be right, as energy never stops flowing,
but the you, the person of this life, is gone. There would be
no reason to mourn the dead if they would still be alive.

There is also no such thing as fate.

Your life is in your own hands.
Yet there will always be inevitable things. Like me.

That is the paradox of being human. You are free in how you live, how you think, how you feel, and yet most of life is out of your control. And weirdly, most of you choose to live in cages made by yourself.

I do understand you, as I am death and have seen you existing since the dawn of your creation and yet, I wonder sometimes…

Every human experience has traits of heaven and hell or however you want to call it. They coexist.

They are no test, they are simply a mirror of the complexity of reality. Have you not felt love and happiness but also grief and desperation while you were one of them?
Have you not lived with the glorious chaos of emotions burned deep into your soul?

Do you see now?
Do you understand?

Yes, some lives are better than others.

Some lives are closer to tragedies while in others the prize
for fulfilled dreams is small. Some humans become villains
while others become saints. Or at least that is what the
world defines them to be. As I said before, evil and holy
do not exist and there is no good person without a shadow
and no traitor without a heart.
But it is true that some suffer more while others find more
elation.

We will talk about this soon.

Have patience, my dear,
I will not keep you waiting for long.

You ask about your connections with people.

If you had listened to me closely you would have
understood that you are connected to everything.
Every drop of water, every bit of oxygen, every animal,
every plant, every human. Yes, all of them.
Even the ones you don't even know exist.
It is that simple.

It is, however, true
that you have more connections to some than to others.

Your family members, your children, your pets, your loved
ones and even some strangers. They are all connected to
you on a deeper level that goes beyond a human lifetime.
They might have been your friends, lovers or enemies in
another life. Maybe someone who saved your life, maybe
your parents from a different timeline.

Not every person you are close to is connected to you
in that way, you are always capable of making new
connections, but some are more deep, like an invisible
thread keeping you together.
You know exactly who I am talking about.

You, dear human soul, are intertwined with them
intimately, you have played a role in each other's life or
even more than one. A bond that reaches through all the
realms, wrapped around the infinite nothingness of the
universe.

We, the gods, smile upon those connections as they are
holy. They are little mirrors of us in you, human one.
Those connections are the closest you humans will come
to the glory of gods.

I cannot tell you if it is love that connects you, as love is beyond the holy. Gods do not interfere with love as it is more powerful than we could ever reveal.

Love and kindness are infinite.

And while it can crumble and fade,
it is indestructible under specific circumstances.

Love can change everything.

Not only for the good, also for the bad, the neutral and the
unknown. It is a force so big only the very substance of a
soul could ever attempt to hold it.

The gods and goddesses of love?

Well, my dear, they do exist but you should rather call them gods and goddesses of romance, friendship, family, desire, longing, intimacy, connection, devotion, adoration, passion, kindness, hope, courage and madness.

Love is beyond us or our control.

Love is wild.
Love is bold.
Love is intangible.

Love is the very substance of the universe.

Brutal. Addictive. Vital. Immortal. Beautiful.

Just like us.
Just like you.
Just like life itself.

Family might not always be what humans would like it to be. What you actually look for is community and belonging. That is where you feel whole.

Family however, those are the people you have connections to. Their function is to teach you lessons. Some are good, some are bad. Some are lessons of love, some are lessons of grief, some are lessons of breaking free.

And you, in return, make them learn lessons as well. Reciprocity, remember?

They are your teachers, but not every teacher is divine.

There is nothing that binds you to them except biological similarities, lessons to learn and your own imagination that tells you that you cannot leave them and create anew. Usually you souls stick to the families you were born into. There is always a reason why you choose them when you enter your life.

But way too many times you end up staying with them simply out of comfort instead of using your inner human sense for exploration and find the belonging you seek somewhere else.

You were lucky this time, human soul, your family gave you a place to be yourself and made you presents of affection and love along the way. But you have seen the destruction a family bond can bring if it is unhealthy and still kept alive.

Yet another lesson about life, my dear, that you need to learn eventually.

Do you think we gods are sticking together because we are related?

No.

We might all be shaped out of the same fabric of this universe, but so are you.

We stick together because we want to.

It is a choice.

Your entire life is a choice.

Which brings me to your final and first choice of all.

Let's retreat into my realm.

Prepare yourself, everything you know will vanish right
here, in the deepest corners of yourself, my dear soul.
Only grief and hope will remain.
And hopefully courage, but that is on you, human one.

Follow me. It is time.

Before you leave, I allow you one last glimpse
at the people and beings of your past life.

Look at them closely.

You will not remember them, but they will remember you.

Like always, when we are about to part, dear human one,
  I grant you a look into the future of the ones you love.

And one sign.

It is overwhelming, I know.

It is good, that you do not feel while you are with me.
The grief and joy, the jealousy and gratitude, the sadness
and hope would be too much for you. To see and
experience so many lives in their fulness, from beginning
to end.

Blurry because nothing is ever certain and yet clear as the
future has all already happened.

But you are with me and therefore, it is okay.

Everything will be okay.

You see their lives laid out for you.

Look closely, dear soul.

Behold.

Observe.
Reflect.
Connect.
Discover.

Be aware.

This is the first and last time you will see with all three
eyes open into what could have been and what will be,
shapes yet to be made, love yet to blossom, scars yet to
form, things yet to vanish and to be born.

Now, pick a sign.

You only get one, because, as I said, we gods do not interfere with humanity. You get to choose one single sign for one being at any point in their lifetime from your death onwards.

Subtle, yet direct,

you are allowed to reach out
and touch their heart
one last time.

.
.
.
.
.
.
.
.

Ah, a wise choice.
I knew you would find your compassion in this last
moment of yourself.

.
.
.

Return your gaze to me now, my dear.
Your past life is over now.
There is no going back.

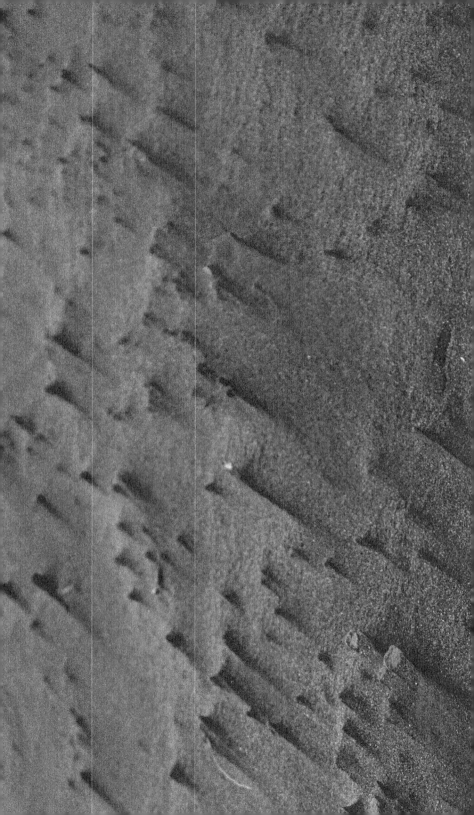

Ah, the sweet scent of emptiness.

A page unwritten, a story untold.

Silence, music to be made.

Stillness, a dance in the making.

Darkness, something to unveil.

Pure light, a morning yet to rise.

There is nothing and there is a road, there is a path. You cannot walk but you move forward, always in motion. There are a billion possibilities but here it is that you choose between you and yourself.

Everything is a question and yet there is only one answer.

Go ahead.

Your next life is awaiting.

A new you is awaiting.

It is time to be reborn as a version of yourself
you have never met, dear human soul.

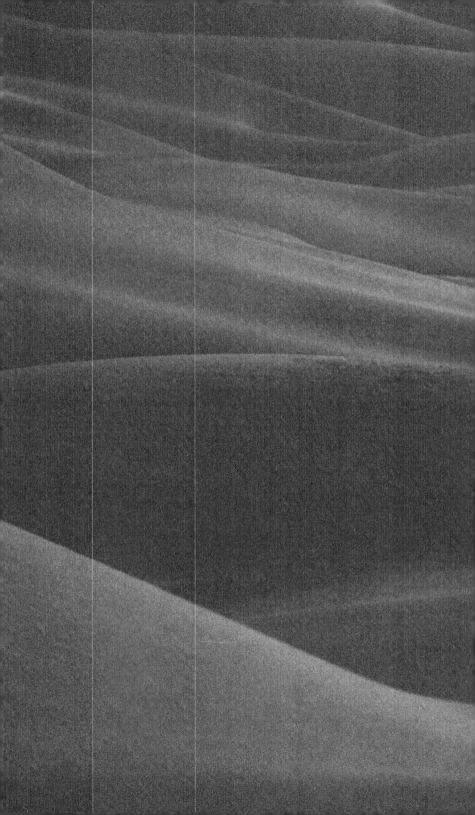

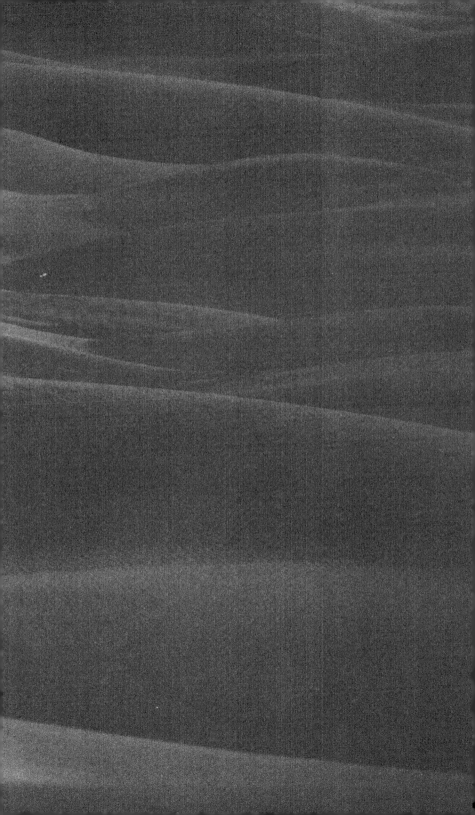

Yes, incarnation.
Or something like it.

We have this conversation every single time you re-enter
my realm. But I am the one who makes you forget.
So, I am not allowed to complain.

You do not get to keep a part of the goddess for yourself.
You have to move on without this knowledge.
And I will explain it to you every single time you return,
forever and ever, like a pendulum of repetition.

No religion, spiritual belief or faith teaches lies
but they do not teach truth either.

They talk about aspects of the truth layered and blurred
with rules made by humans to create community and
remain control. They are the relics of your time in the
nowhere, with me. They are the echoes our interaction
leaves behind.

Every preacher tries to get closer to the unsolved mystery,
yet by preaching alone they go astray. Every believer tries
their best but loses themselves by thinking they have done
enough or know it all. Every holy text carries a fragment of
the truth yet is meaningless in regards to reality.

It is so much bigger than that.

Your religions are the ruins of long forgotten dynasties of dreams, awoken in the shadows of death and ecstasy.

The only way to experience truth is to be one with all life on earth and since that is impossible while you are ... well you, human soul, you only learn about it with me.

And I do not allow you to keep this wisdom until you have made the circle complete and have understood all of this by yourself.

Remember what I said about your ideas of heaven and hell?

Well, now it is on me to send you off into a direction that reflects the lessons you need to learn most.

It is a complex game, far more than your being could handle. There is so much to consider, yet it is as easy as bringing you here.

Sending someone off is just as hard and just as simple as letting someone in.

The final decisions are always yours to make.

There are options laid out for you, burned into the core of
your existence and once you move towards one of them,
life will unfold for you once again.

There will be no return
except for greeting me yet again at the end of it all.

I do not owe you answers but I allow you one last question.

.

.

.

Oh my dear human soul, I can tell you are getting old.

You have finally asked a question before jumping into the abyss of a new beginning.

Yes, my dear, your guess was right.

.

You are whole, you are all, you are flow.

.

Every living being on this planet is you in a different incarnation. Every plant you rip out of the ground, every tree you set on fire, every animal you eat, every bug you poison, every pet you love, every person you ever hurt and everyone who has ever hurt you, every bully, every saviour, every lover, every stranger.

It is all you, dear human soul.

Do you understand now, why love and kindness should be
your compass in a world without orientation?

Not because it gains you favours or because of karma.
No.
Because the proverb stating that

.

the love you give will always return to you

.

is the only truth you have put into words as of yet.

It will take a lot more lives before you finally realize that by yourself. And when you do, there are other truths to unveil, some of which I have shared with you today.

You, dear soul, will expand, over time.

But not linear, oh no.
That is a human concept you, too, will need to shake off.

Right now, you could become an animal raised for food,
you could become the seed to a century old tree, you could
become a woman in ancient times, a trans person in a time
before colonialism, your own mother from your last life,
someone from the future, a pet of someone you never met,
a wild cat from the forest, a warrior of a forgotten empire,
a dinosaur watching the meteor, a fungi between roots, a
sea creature deep in the ocean, a world leader, your worst
enemy, your one true love.

No matter where or how or who. You will start small,
you will grow, you will learn, you will return. I am your
beginning, I am your end, but you...

.

You are everyone.
And everything.
From the first cell to the last.

You, my dear soul, are *life*.

.
.

And now, it is time to embrace yourself.

. . .
.
.
.
. . . . .
.
.
.
. . .

Let go of this realm.

.
.
.

So, one day we shall meet as equals.

ACKNOWLEDGMENTS

As stated in the dedication, this book is for the roots of my family tree. It is also for everyone who has ever had to deal with the monster called grief or with the fear of death.

Further, I would like to thank João for believing in me, listening to all the first bizarre drafts and letting me express my emotions in this dark, twisted form that turned into a book that hopefully makes someone out there feel seen or touched. I love you, batata.

A special thank you goes to my wonderful friend Sky who corrected my grammar, ~~even tho~~ even though it was an odd text and you were so busy. You are truly wonderful!

Big hugs and my gratitude go to Filipa, Mona, Stephie and Tobi and my other friends for supporting me every step of the way. All of you have shown me grief in unique perspectives and have therefore inspired this book. And to Nina who gave me the best head massage while I spent days upon days on my laptop, piecing this book together.

Of course, I also have to thank my beautiful island, its nature, its magic and its people as well as the ocean. You are my home, you are my everything.

Lastly, I would like to thank each and every single one of my readers who have supported my debut, *The Anatomy of Waves* and who now hold *Welcome Home, Dear Soul* in their hands. I am beyond grateful.

In the end

This is for all life that has passed. Every living being that has ever touched the world. I am sorry you had to leave, but your energy is still here, cycling through all of us, never lost, never forgotten. You are all our ancestors. Immortal and loved.

This is for everyone who is in pain over the loss of someone or something they loved. Your grief is valid. Healing takes times and strength and courage and patience and is never fully complete. But even with those scars and those tears, you will always be whole. And never, ever alone.

This is for the planet. I am sorry you have to endure our human ways of destruction and ignorance. I am sorry your air tastes bitter, your oceans carry plastic and your forests disappear. I am so, so, so sorry. Believe me, that some of us are trying to make it better, but we all know it might not be enough or it might be too late. We love you, Mother Earth. We truly do. My heart is broken with you, while I plant flowers and seeds into the soil of the future.

ABOUT THE AUTHOR

Tasmin Hansmann is a storyteller, writer, poet and earth child. Born and raised in Munich, Germany, she found herself a new home on the Azores Archipelago where she is currently living. She works as a freelance writer and is the founder of Azorean Stories.

Her first book *The Anatomy of Waves* is a poetry collection about the healing of trauma and the beauty of the Azores Archipelago. It was released in 2021.

More:

tasmin-hansmann.de

azorean-stories.com

Printed in Great Britain
by Amazon

66154445R00098